Bug Boy
Slug
Picnic

T0385961

Written by Jeanne Willis
Illustrated by Ben Mantle

Dan had lots of pet bugs.

He had bugs in jars and bugs in tubs.

He had red bugs, green bugs, fat bugs and thin bugs.

red bugs

green bugs

fat bugs

thin bugs

Dan liked Sid best. Sid was a slug.

Dan put Sid in a tin. He put some slug food in, too.

"Come on, Sid. We are going on a picnic," said Dan.

Mum got the picnic out.

"Dan's roll is bigger than my roll," said Emma.
"No, it's not," said Dan.

Dan got Sid's tin out.
He took the lid off.

But Sid was not there!

Dan went to look for Sid.
"Now I can have the
big roll!" said Emma.

But Sid was in the roll!

"Yuck! A big slug!"
yelled Emma.

15

"There you are, Sid," said Dan. "Eat up!"